CALVARY'S LOVE *Story*

An Inspirational Easter Celebration

Arranged and Orchestrated by
NICK ROBERTSON

lillenas
PUBLISHING COMPANY
lillenas.com

Copyright © 2019 by Lillenas Publishing Company, Box 419527, Kansas City, MO 64141. All rights reserved.
Litho in U.S.A.

CONTENTS

Easter Medley 3
    Christ Is Risen
    Christ the Lord Is Risen Today
    Crown Him with Many Crowns

Here He Comes 16

I Will Follow *with* Where He Leads Me 28

Calvary's Love 36

He Lives *with* O How I Love Jesus 45

If You Knew Him 56

Here He Comes (reprise) 70

Easter Medley

Includes: *Christ Is Risen, Christ the Lord Is Risen Today,
and Crown Him with Many Crowns*

Arranged by Nick Robertson

*CD POINTS: Split-channel, CD: 1-41; Split-channel for performance narration, CD: 42-48

*Words and Music by Matt Maher and Mia Fieldes. Copyright © 2009 Thankyou Music (PRS) (adm. worldwide at CapitolCMGPublishing.com excluding Europe which is adm. by Integrity Music, part of the David C Cook family). Songs@integritymusic.com) / SpiritandSong.Com Pub (BMI) (adm. at CapitolCMGPublishing.com) / Upside Down Under (BMI) Be Essential Songs (BMI) (admin at EssentialMusicPublishing.com). All rights reserved. Used by permission.

PLEASE NOTE: The copying of this music is prohibited by law and is not covered by CCLI or OneLicense.net.

wake! Come and rise up from the grave! Come and

rise up from the grave! Rise up from the grave!

Rise up from the grave!

cresc.

* "Christ the Lord Is Risen Today"

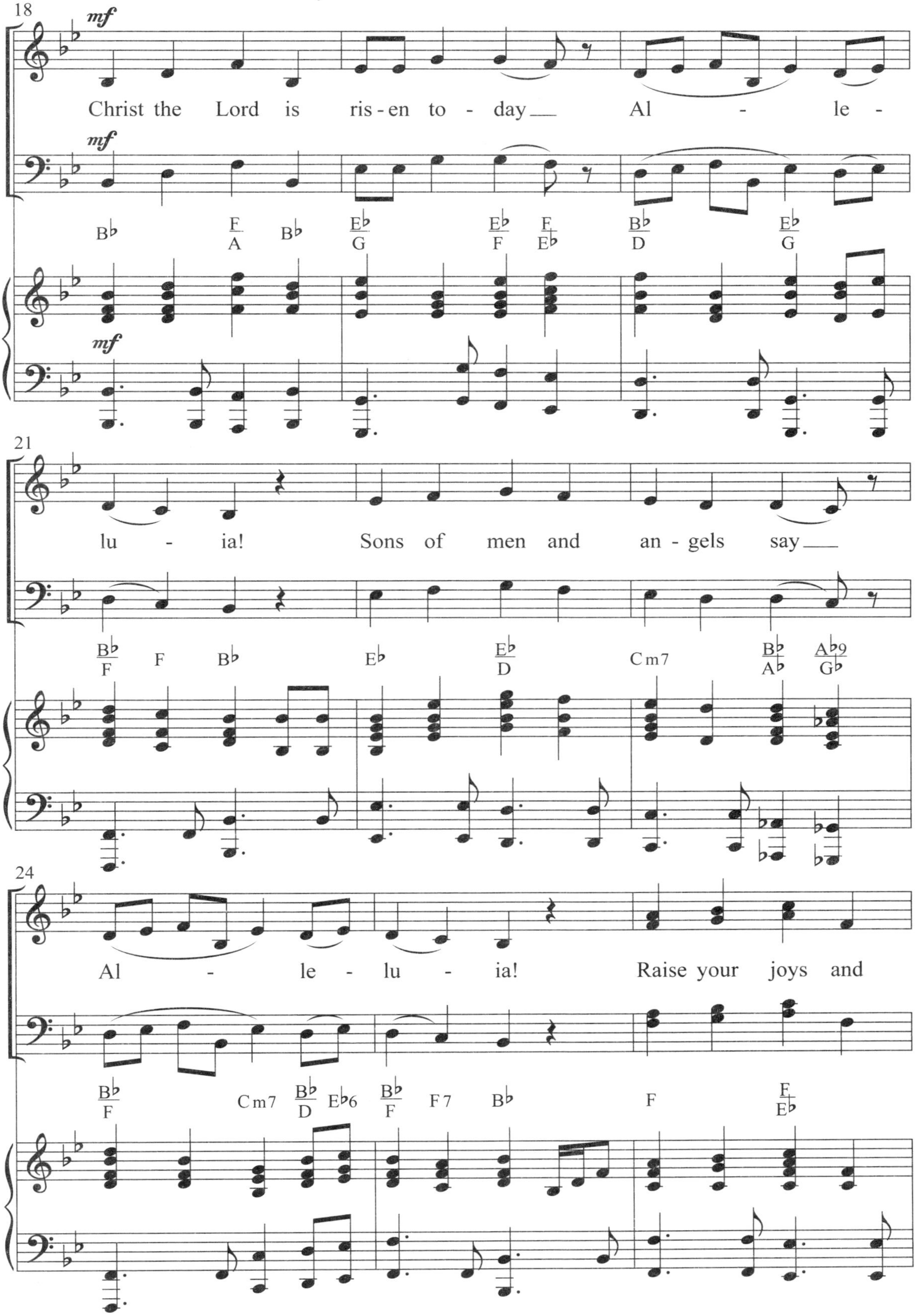

tri - umphs high! Al - le - lu - ia! Sing ye heav'ns and earth re - ply Al - le - lu - ia!

* "Crown Him with Many Crowns"

Crown Him with man-y crowns! The Lamb up-on His throne. Hark! How the heav'n-ly an-them drowns all

*Words - Matthew Bridges / M - George J. Elvey. Arr. © 2019 Pilot Point Music (ASCAP) (admin. by Music Services). All rights reserved.

45
mu - sic but its own. A - wake my soul and
A♭ D♭2 E♭sus E♭ A♭sus A♭/G♭ D♭/F E♭m7 D♭
48
sing, of Him, Who died for
G♭ G♭/E E♭ D♭2/F E♭/G
50
thee! And hail Him as thy
A♭ B♭m A♭ G♭ D♭/F

matchless King, through all e - ter - ni - ty! Crown Him the Lord of Life! Who tri - umphed o'er the grave; Who rose vic - to - rious

to the strife for those He came to save. His glo-ries now we sing Who died and rose on high, Who died e-ter-nal life to bring, And lives that death may die! Who died e-ter-nal life to bring, And lives that death may die! O death, where is your sting?

O hell, where is your victory? O Church, come stand in the light. The glory of God has defeated the night! Singin'

O death, where is your sting? O hell, where is your vic-to-ry? O Church, come stand in the light. Our God is not dead! He's a-live! He's a-live! Christ is ris - en from the dead! Tramp-ling o - ver death by death! Come a-wake! Come a - wake! Come and rise up from the grave! Christ is ris - en from the dead! We are one with Him a - gain! Come a -

wake! Come a - wake! Come and rise up from the grave! Come a

A   C#m7   B

wake! Come a - wake! Come and rise up from the grave!

F#m7   AMaj7   B

Come a - wake!

E

Here He Comes

Words and Music by
TONY WOOD, CHRIS CRON
and JOSEPH HABEDANK
Arranged by Nick Robertson

43 NARRATION: There is no other name under heaven that stirs the heart of mankind like the Name of Jesus. From Bethlehem's manger to Calvary's cross, His journey was marked by a measure of love and compassion the world had never experienced. He was a man on a mission, come to seek and save a people walking in darkness. And into a world that knew Him not, this Redeemer came. *(Music begins)* After centuries of waiting, Scripture tells us a host of heaven's angels gathered in the midnight skies with a long-awaited announcement. Christ the Lord has come!

Joyous (♩ = 135)

CHOIR *unison*

Here He comes step-

Copyright © 2016 Tony Wood Songs (SESAC) (admin. by Wordspring Music, LLC) / Christian Taylor Music (BMI) Winding Way Music (ASCAP)
Crondor Music (ASCAP) (admin. by ClearBox Rights, LLC). All rights reserved. Used by permission.

PLEASE NOTE: The copying of this music is prohibited by law and is not covered by CCLI or OneLicense.net.

-pin' down from glory. Beth-le-hem, just the start of the story. Here He comes.

Oh, here He comes.

18

Here He comes, teach - ing in the tem - ple

mak - in' time - less wis - dom sound sim - ple.

Here He comes. Oh,

here He comes. Here He comes to seek and save, to wash our ev-er-y sin a-way. Hear the cap-

-tives start to say, "Here He comes!" Here He comes giving sight to a blind man. Calling out, giving life to a dead man Here He comes.

Oh, here He comes.

Here He comes, "Ho - san - nas" loud - ly ring - ing.

Car - ries the cross a - long the way of suf - fring.

Here He comes. Oh, here He comes.

G♭2　　　　　　　　　　　　　　　D♭

Here He comes to seek and save,

A♭(no3)

to wash our ev - er - y sin a - way.

Bbm

Hear the cap - tives start to say,

Cb2

"Here He comes!"

Gb2   Absus

Here He comes, a mir-a-cle at sun-rise.

An emp-ty tomb is shout-ing He's a-live

Here He comes. Oh, here He comes.

25

Here He comes. Oh glor-ious day, He is ris-en from the grave. All cre-a-tion shouts His praise,

12
70
"Here He comes!"
Here He comes!
G2
Asus
73
Here He
Bm
75
comes!
Here He comes!
C
G
D

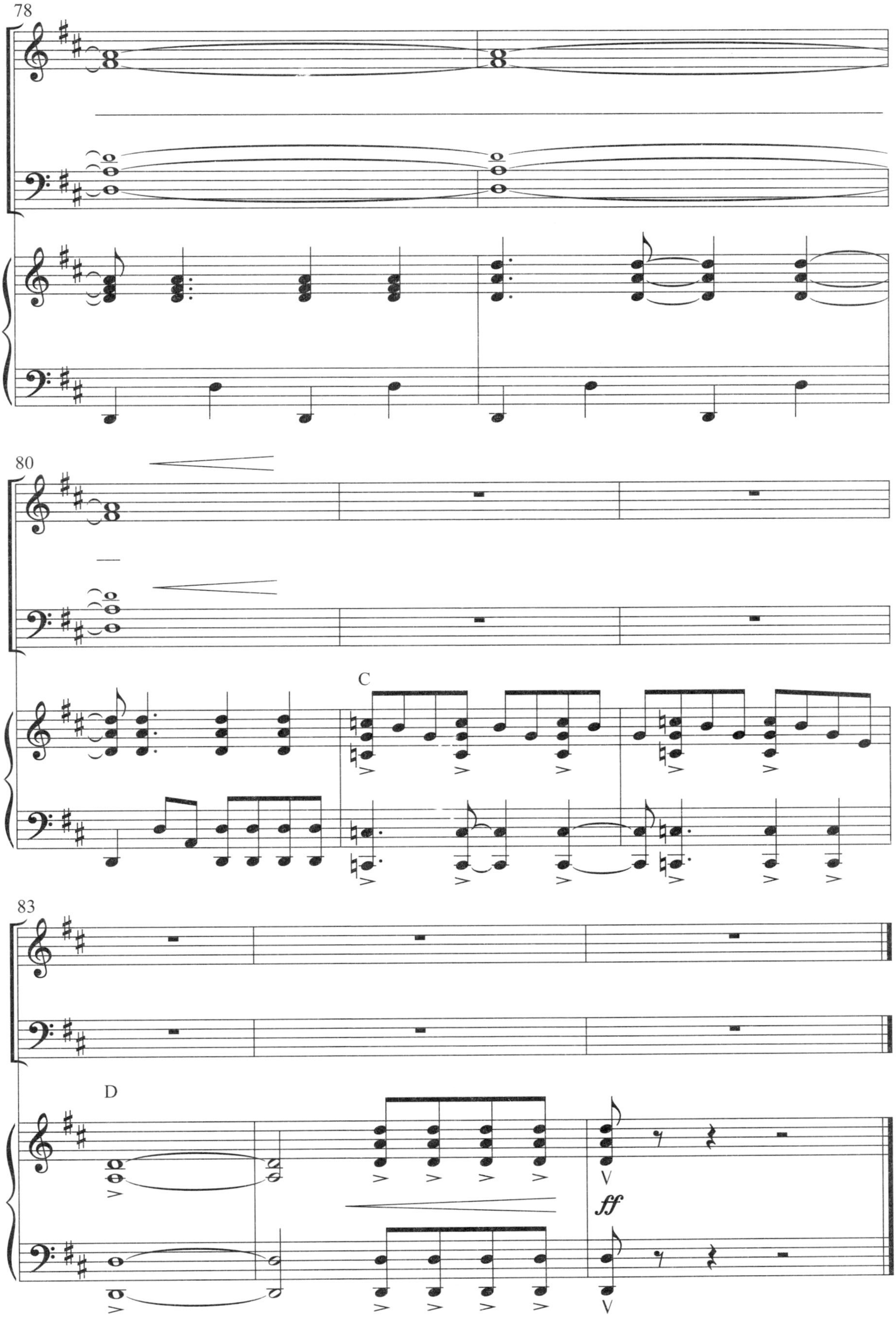
78
80
C
83
D
ff

I Will Follow

with Where He Leads Me

Words and Music by
DAVE CLARK and NICK ROBERTSON
Arranged by Nick Robertson

44 NARRATOR: *As Jesus walked beside the Sea of Galilee, he saw Simon and his brother Andrew casting a net into the lake. Jesus called out to the fishermen with what to some may have sounded like a simple request. "Come, follow me, and I will make you fishers of men." With a response revealing trust without question and surrender without reservation, Scripture tells us they left their nets behind and followed.

Tenderly (♩ = 60)
*Narration begins

CHOIR unison

I will fol-low

Copyright © 2019 Pilot Point Music (ASCAP) PsalmSinger Music (BMI) Shakertown Road Music (BMI)
Sunday Best Music (ASCAP) (admin. by Music Services). All rights reserved.

PLEASE NOTE: The copying of this music is prohibited by law and is not covered by CCLI or OneLicense.net.

You, this road from Beth-le-hem. A-long the dus-ty streets un-to Je-ru-sa-lem. You can calm a rag-ing storm and feed a mul-ti-tude, still You call to me. I will fol-low You. I will fol-low You and hear the words You speak. Teach-er to the wise, a Shep-herd to the sheep. There's a King-dom to be

*"Where He Leads Me"

*Words by E.W. Blandy, Music by John S. Norris. Arr. © 2019 Pilot Point Music (ASCAP) (admin. by Music Services). All rights reserved.

32

lead me I will fol - low. I'll go with You, with You,

all the way. Where You

lead me I will fol - low. Where You lead me I will

42
fol - low. Where You lead me I will fol - low. I'll go
A/B Bm Am7 D13 Am/G G Gm/B♭
45
with You, with You, all the way.
D/A A7sus G2/A Bm F♯m/A GMaj7 D2/F♯
48
17
mp
I will fol - low
mp
FMaj7 G/F Fmaj7 G/F Em7(4)
8va
f
mf

You on crucifixion day; The thorns upon Your brow, the price You chose to pay. When I see You on the cross and all that You went through, how can I give

57
less? I will fol - low You. Lord, I will not turn
D/A
A7sus
Bm
DMaj7/A
G
Em7
59
back, I will fol - low You.
D/A
A7sus
N.C.
62
rit.
a tempo
65
D

Calvary's Love

Words and Music by
PHIL McHUGH and GREG NELSON
Arranged by Nick Robertson

45 NARRATOR: On the night before Jesus was betrayed, He gathered with the twelve in the upper room. Even as He tried to tell them His hour was at hand, they could not understand. But in the days and hours that followed, God's redemption plan would be revealed in all its glory. The prayer in Gethsemane, the betrayal of Judas, the arrest, the trial . . . It was all happening so quickly. *(Music begins)* A scarlet robe, a crown of thorns, the agony of a Roman cross. And then with one final cry of surrender, it was finished.

LADIES *unis.*

Cal - v'ry's

Copyright © 1986 Greg Nelson Music (BMI) River Oaks Music Company (BMI) Universal Music - Brentwood Benson Songs (BMI) (adm. at CapitolCMGPublishing.com). All rights reserved. Used by permission.

PLEASE NOTE: The copying of this music is prohibited by law and is not covered by CCLI or OneLicense.net.

love will sail for-ev-er, bright and shin-ing, strong and free. Like an ark of peace and safe-ty on the sea of hu-man need. Through the hours of all the ag-es,___ those tired of sail-ing on their own, fin-'lly rest_____ in-side the shad-ow___ cast by Cal-v'ry's love a-cross their soul._____ Cal-v'ry's

27
love, Cal-v'ry's love, price-less
Fm Cm7 A♭/C
mf
29
gift Christ makes us wor-thy of; The deep-est sin can't rise a-
D♭ E♭ A♭ A♭ E♭/G Fm Fm/E♭
32
bove Cal-v'ry's love.
B♭/D Cm7 B♭ B♭/A♭ G♭ E♭sus E♭

Cal-v'ry's love can heal the spir-it life has crushed and cast a-side; And re-deem 'til heav-en's prom-ise fills with

joy once emp-ty eyes. So de-sire to tell the sto-ry of a love that loved e-nough to die. burns a-way all oth-er pas-sions and fed by Cal-v'ry's

love be-comes a fire. Cal-v'ry's love, Cal-v'ry's love, price-less gift Christ makes us wor-thy of; The deep-est sin can't rise a-

bove Cal-v'ry's love. Cal-v'ry's love, Cal-v'ry's love, price-less gift Christ makes us wor-thy of; The deep-est sin can't rise a-bove Cal-v'ry's love. Cal-v'ry's love! Cal-v'ry's love! Cal - v'ry's love!

He Lives

with
O How I Love Jesus

Words and Music by
ALFRED HENRY ACKLEY
Arranged by Nick Robertson

46 NARRATOR: It was early in the morning on the first day of the week when Mary and the others came to the tomb with spices they had prepared. When they arrived, they saw the stone guarding the entrance was no longer there. *(Music begins)* But an angel appeared and said to them, "Don't be afraid, this Jesus you are looking for is no longer here. He has risen, just like He said."

26 **Gospel Style** (♩ = 82)

CHOIR *unis.*

I serve a ris-en Sav-ior, He's in the world to-day. I

Copyright © 1933, renewed 1961 The Rodeheaver Co. (ASCAP) (admin. by Word Music, LLC). All rights reserved. Used by permission.

PLEASE NOTE: The copying of this music is prohibited by law and is not covered by CCLI or OneLicense.net.

know that He is liv - ing, what - ev - er men may say. I see His hand of mer - cy, I hear His voice of cheer; And just the time I need Him, He's al - ways near. He

15
lives! He lives! Christ Je - sus lives to - day! He
G7 C/G G C7 G7
17
walks with me and talks with me a - long life's nar - row way. He
Am7 D7/F♯ Em7 A7 D7 F7 F♯7
19
lives! He lives! Sal - va - tion to im - part! You
G7 C7 B7

48

ask me how I know He lives? He lives with-in my heart!

Re-

joice, re-joice, O Christian! Lift up your voice and sing e-ter-nal hal-le-lu-jahs to Je-sus Christ, the King! The Hope of all who seek Him, the Help of all who find, None oth-er is so lov-ing, so good and kind. He lives! He lives! Christ Je-sus lives to-day! He walks with me and talks with me a-long life's nar-row way. He

*Words by Frederick Whitfield, Music: Traditional American Melody. Arr. © 2019 Pilot Point Music (ASCAP) (admin. by Music Services) All rights reserved.

Je - sus! O how I love Je - sus! O how I love Je - sus! Be - cause He first loved me! O how I love Je - sus!

56
O how I love Je - sus! O how I love
Em7 A7 F9(♯11) Cm6/E♭ G/D CMaj7
mf
59
Je - sus! Be - cause He first loved me! Be -
G2/B Dm13 G9 Am7 G/B C G/D D7 G Em7
62
32
cause He first loved me! Be -
Am7 G/B C G/D D7 G Em7
2/4

64
cresc.
ff
cause ___ He lives! He lives! Christ Je-sus lives to - day! He
Am7 G/B C
Ab/C Ab Db7 Ab7
67
walks with me and talks with me a - long life's nar-row way. He
Bbm7 Eb7/G Fm7 Bb7 Eb7 Gb7 G7
69
lives! He lives! Sal - va - tion to im - part! You
Ab7 Db7 C7

ask me how I know He lives? _____ He lives with - in my heart! He lives! _____

If You Knew Him

Words and Music by
RODNEY GRIFFIN and JOSEPH HABEDANK
Arranged by Nick Robertson

NARRATOR: For two thousand years believers have celebrated the power of the empty tomb. We come with our sins and shame, failures and regrets, and lay them all at the feet of Jesus. But just like His story did not end at the cross, our story doesn't end there either. For the cross is more than just what Jesus did, it is the life He invites us to. *(Music begins)* We have been called to a covenant journey with the King of kings and Lord of lords. To experience for ourselves the glory of who He is and who He came to be.

Ballad (♩ = 60)

MALE SOLO

I walked by the tomb of Buddha, looked inside and saw his bones. Traveled on to see Mu-

Copyright © 2009 Christian Taylor Music (BMI) (admin. by ClearBox Rights, LLC) / Songs of Greater Vision (BMI) (admin. by rodneygriffin@me.com). All rights reserved. Used by permission.

PLEASE NOTE: The copying of this music is prohibited by law and is not covered by CCLI or OneLicense.net.

57

ham - mad still wrapped up in his grave clothes. Then I jour - neyed to a gar - den, where old Jo - seph left Him lain. The pre - cious Lamb, God's own be - got - ten, was no

34
19
long - er in that grave. If you
CHOIR parts
mf
If you
mf
E/B
B7sus
B7
E
21
knew Him like I know Him, you would
knew Him like I know Him, you would
B
B/A
A
A/E
E
mf

59

know___ that He's a - live! If you

know___ that He's a - live! If you

felt___ Him like I feel___ Him. Res - ur -

felt___ Him like I feel___ Him. Res - ur -

rec - tion, deep in - side_____ You'd know He's

rec - tion, deep in - side_____ You'd know He's

liv - ing, and death has died. If you're

liv - ing, and death has died.

wan-d'ring in the dark-ness, come and step in-to the light. Nail-scarred hands_____ reach out to help____ you, to pull you

safe from death to life. Friend, I too____ have stood where

Ooo____

63

36
45
f
love He ran to me!
f
If you
f
E/B
B7sus
B7
E
47
Knew Him. Like I know Him
3
knew Him like I know Him, you would
B
B/A
A
A/E
E
f

that He's a - live! and if You
know___ that He's a - live! If you

felt___ Him like I feel___ Him. Res - ur -
felt___ Him like I feel___ Him. Res - ur -

rec - tion, deep in - side _____ You'd know He's

rec - tion, deep in - side _____ You'd know He's

E/B   E B/D# C#m   E7/B   A

37

liv - ing, and death has died! You

liv - ing, and death has died! You

E/B   B7sus   E   E/D

ask me how I know He lives, He

ask me how I know He lives, He

C Gm7 G♭7 FMaj7 F6 Am/F♯

lives, with-in my heart! If you

lives, with-in my heart!

C/G Asus/E A

felt ___ Him like I feel ___ Him. Res - ur -

felt ___ Him like I feel ___ Him. Res - ur -

rec - tion, deep in - side ___ You'd know He's

rec - tion, deep in - side ___ You'd know He's

66
liv - ing, and death has died!
liv - ing, and death has died!
D/A
A 7sus
D
D/C
Gm/B♭
D/A
68
rit.
a tempo
Death has died!
rit.
a tempo
Death has died!
Gm
Gm/F
Gm/E
Gm/A
D
D/A
D
D/A
D
rit.
a tempo

Here He Comes (Reprise)

Words and Music by
TONY WOOD, CHRIS CRON
and JOSEPH HABEDANK
Arranged by Nick Robertson

Joyous (♩ = 135)

CHOIR *parts*

Here He comes! ___ Oh glor-ious day,

Copyright © 2016 Tony Wood Songs (SESAC) (admin. by Wordspring Music, LLC) / Christian Taylor Music (BMI) Winding Way Music (ASCAP)
Crondor Music (ASCAP) (admin. by ClearBox Rights, LLC). All rights reserved. Used by permission.

PLEASE NOTE: The copying of this music is prohibited by law and is not covered by CCLI or OneLicense.net.

He is ris-en from the grave

Bm7

All cre-a-tion shouts His praise,

C

"Here He comes!"

G2   Asus

My heart beats with expectation.

My soul aches with anticipation.

Oh what a moment of celebration when we

see Him in the sky!

Here He comes, step - ping down from glo - ry!

Com - ing back to fin - ish the sto - ry

74

Here He comes! — Oh, here He comes! — Here He comes, and I can't wait for the dawn-

-ing of that day, ____ when the an-

-gels fin - 'lly say, ____ "Here He comes!" __

41

_____ Here He comes! _____

Here He comes! Here He comes!